**Six simple steps that will help you
fulfill your child's potential for
success and happiness.**

Symptoms checklist:

- Do you find yourself doing things yourself because it's easier than trying to get your children to do it?

- Do you have to nag your children to get them to do their chores or homework?

- Do they have the potential to get better grades?

- Are your children struggling to balance school with sports and other activities?

- Do you find less and less time for family time?

- Is your time together less enjoyable than you'd like?

If you answered yes to any one of these questions, you and your kids will benefit from this book!

Benefits to realize:

- Children achieve better grades with less effort.

- Children gain self-esteem.

- Parents and kids enjoy their time together more.

- Children understand and accept their boundaries.

- Children have more free time for the things they enjoy.

- Develops a caring, team atmosphere at home.

- Eliminates frustration for everyone.

- Children fulfill their potential.

Help Your Kids Get it Done Right at Home and School!

Building Responsibility &
Self-Esteem in Children

by
Donna M. Genett, Ph.D.

Sanger, California

Printed in the United States of America

Published by Quill Driver Books/Word Dancer Press, Inc.
1254 Commerce Avenue
Sanger, California 93657
559-876-2170 • 800-497-4909 • FAX 559-876-2180
QuillDriverBooks.com
Info@QuillDriverBooks.com

Quill Driver Books titles may be purchased in quantity at special discounts for educational, inservice, fund-raising, training, business, or promotional use. Please contact Special Markets, Quill Driver Books/Word Dancer Press, Inc. at the above address, toll-free at 1-800-497-4909, or by e-mail: Info@QuillDriverBooks.com

Quill Driver Books/Word Dancer Press, Inc. project cadre:
Mary Ann Gardner, Joshua Blake Mettee, Stephen Blake Mettee, Tom Tidyman

First printing

ISBN 1-884956-45-9

To order another copy of this book, please call
1-800-497-4909

Library of Congress Cataloging-in-Publication Data

Genett, Donna M., 1955-

Help your kids get it done right at home and school! : building responsibility & self-esteem in children / by Donna M. Genett.

p. cm.

ISBN 1-884956-45-9 (Hardcover.)

1. Child rearing. 2. Parenting. 3. Parent and child. I. Title.

HQ769.G3945 2005

649'.7--dc22

2005003978

Contents

Introduction

$\mathbf{M}$y first book, *If You Want It Done Right, You **Don't** Have to Do It Yourself!,* was written to address a widespread need I discovered as an executive coach. Many managers I coach have never been taught the fundamental steps of effective delegation. Although they are expected to delegate, and, although effective delegation is critical to their professional success and personal quality of life, there are few venues for them to learn delegation skills.

Colleagues and friends who read *If You Want It Done Right, You **Don't** Have to Do It Yourself!* brought to my attention that these skills are extremely relevant for parents as well as managers. *Help Your Kids Get It Done Right at Home and School! Building Responsibility and Self-Esteem in Children* translates the steps of effective delegation into a format that is immediately applicable for parents interested in helping their children achieve their highest potential for success and happiness.

In *If You Want It Done Right, You **Don't** Have to Do It Yourself!,* James struggled as he compared his mediocre professional performance and impaired quality of life with his cousin's top-notch management skills and strong, rewarding home life. James's pain increased to a point where he finally swallowed his pride and approached his cousin for some much-needed advice. By following the guidance he received from his cousin, James gradually learned the steps of effective delegation and achieved masterful delegation status with all its benefits.

In *Help Your Kids Get It Done Right at Home and School!,* James recognizes that the gap between his performance and that of Jones's extends beyond their management skills. Jones is a better father as well. So, once again, James sets out to discover Jones's secrets.

○ **1** ○

Meet Jones and James:
So Alike, So Different

John Jones, Jr. and John James, Jr. weren't typical cousins. They grew up in the same town, on the same street, next door to each other. Their mothers were identical twins and best friends who married John Jones and John James at about the same time. Amazingly, the two men had also grown up as best friends. Even more amazingly, the two John Juniors arrived on the same day, in the same hospital, with their mothers sharing a semi-private room.

Because four Johns in such close proximity creates confusion, the boys were called Jones and

James inside the family. In time, everyone else used these nicknames, too.

No one knew if their similarities were caused by identical-twin mothers. It didn't matter. The cousins looked and acted like twins. Before they were in kindergarten, they had discovered the art of deliberately confusing family and friends. In elementary school, they perfected it. In high school, they spent almost all their free time together, took the same classes, and played the same sports. They were equally matched as both students and athletes.

The cousins attended the same college and continued to show up in the same classes. They took some flak about it, but anyone who was paying attention could see that they weren't doing it out of some kind of dependence. The truth was they genuinely enjoyed the same things and got a kick out of doing them in tandem, so to speak.

After college, they continued the tradition of amazing everyone (at this point, no one was really surprised—just amused and curious) by marrying twin sisters in a double ceremony. They started families at the same time. They took jobs in the same company and mortgages on houses on the same block. What's more, they both did their jobs well. Everyone was happy. Things were looking good.

And they *were* good, too, until Jones and James were both promoted into management. It didn't take James long to notice that for the first time they were not duplicates of each other. There was definitely a difference. It wasn't a little difference. And worse yet, it was growing!

Luckily James saw the difference when he did. Even more to his credit, he was able to swallow his pride enough to seek and follow his cousin's advice. It turned out that the biggest difference they ever encountered between them was due to the power of effective delegation. Once James learned how to delegate more effectively, thanks to Jones's instruction, the differences between them started to diminish. Soon James started reaping the benefits of effective delegation too.

Recently, however, James became aware of another difference between himself and Jones. As his delegation skills were improved and perfected, James was able to spend more time with his family. What he saw surprised and scared him.

Jones and James had started their families around the same time so their children were very close in age. In fact, their two sons, Joe and Jake, were born just one day apart, and their two daughters, Jamie and Jolie, were born one week apart. The two boys were in the ninth grade, and the girls were in the sixth grade.

Jones's children, Joe and Jamie, were doing great in school. They completed their assignments without complaint. After finishing their homework, they had time left over for their favorite sports. James's children, Jake and Jolie, on the other hand, were struggling in school. And for the first time, their ability to remain on the basketball and soccer teams was in question because of their academic struggles. This development was breaking their hearts, which they expressed as frustration and anger. James wanted to nip these developments in the bud before things really got out of hand.

He started by watching the Jones family more closely. He was embarrassed to spy this way, but he knew he would be able to learn from Jones. He noticed that Jones spent quite a bit of time with Joe and Jamie. Weekday evenings they were usually all outside together. James and Joe shot hoops, while Jamie practiced her cartwheels and got an occasional spot from Jones for a walkover or handspring.

On Saturday mornings the whole family seemed to pitch in to get the chores done. The afternoon was then spent having fun. James noticed something else, too. When Jones helped the kids with something, he had a unique way of doing so. James couldn't quite put his finger on what it was, but it was definitely different from what he did with his own kids.

James contrasted the Jones family interactions with those of his own. As he thought about it, he wondered why he didn't spend time with his children the way Jones did. He knew it used to be because his work consumed him, but those days were gone now that he learned how to delegate effectively. This had changed his life at work and at home; at least he now had much more time with his family. But as he thought about it, he realized that while he had more time with his family, the *quality* of that time was relatively unchanged.

The weekday ritual involved James and his wife, Joyce, making dinner after they got home from work.

The family would sit down together as often as possible to eat and talk about their days. Then he and Joyce would clear the table and do the dishes while the kids went to do their homework. After that, they would read the paper or watch television until it was time for the kids to go to bed.

Why was it, he wondered, that his family had no play time together in the evening? Why was it that, although Jake and Jolie spent more time studying, they were not doing as well in school as Jones's kids?

On the weekends, he and Joyce struggled with the kids to get them to help with chores. The procrastination and antagonistic exchanges often chewed up much of the day. How did Jones get his children to not only help out but to seem to enjoy doing so? Why was the Jones family so efficient and effective at the "work" that they had loads of free time for play? These questions and more began plaguing James. He became intent on learning more about what was so different between their families.

° 2 °

James Tells a Story

Saturday morning, James made a point of stopping by his cousin's house. He did it in the guise of delivering an invitation for them to come over for a cook-out, but he really wanted to see just how Jones's family operated. His reactions to what he observed were a mixture of awe, confusion, and excitement. Awe that things with the kids could run so smoothly, confusion as to how such an environment was created, and excitement about the hope of generating such a spirit of cooperation within his own family.

"Hey, Jonsey, what's happening over here this

fine Saturday morning?" were his first words after walking in.

"Hi!" the Joneses cried in unison. They were just finishing breakfast.

"What's up with you?" Jones asked him, "How are you spending your day off?"

"Well, I hope to spend it cooking up a storm for the Jones family!" he exclaimed. "Want to come over for dinner tonight?"

"Yeah!" the kids shouted. Since the four kids were all best friends, any chance to spend time together was welcomed.

"Who can argue with that?" Jones smiled and looked at his wife, Jane, who nodded in agreement. "Guess we have a date."

As they talked, James noted what was going on. Joe was clearing the table without being asked. Jamie was filling the sink with water in preparation for doing the dishes, also without being asked. Amazing. Whether they were asked, told, cajoled, or commanded, James's kids resisted doing any chores. Curious as he was, he couldn't help but blurt out what was on his mind.

"Good for you two, pitching in to help without even being asked."

"We're a part of the team!" they exclaimed.

"The team, eh?" James asked, shooting Jones a quizzical look.

Jones just smiled and shrugged. He was picking up that James was doing some exploration. After all, he'd been down this path with James before and knew him well.

"Yeah," Jamie explained, "our family is a team, just like my soccer team at school. We all have things we're best at and what we like best, so we each do our part to be the best team we can be." She could hardly contain her enthusiasm, and it was definitely contagious.

"Pretty progressive thinking for a sixth grader," James thought. He wondered how the Jones family ever got to this point. "Wow, that's really neat," he said.

"Is your family a team too?" Jamie asked.

Out of the mouths of babes. "Well," he stammered, "I guess we are, but I don't think we're as good a team as you are. We're working on it though." At least they soon would be, he thought to himself. But where would he start? That would be a conversation to have with Jones.

Jones must have read his mind. "James," he said, "could you give me a hand in the garage?"

"Okay, what gives?" James queried as they walked into the garage shutting the door behind them.

"Well, it's really pretty simple." Jones replied. "You see, we were having a lot of trouble getting the kids to accept responsibility. Then one day, when I was watching Joe's coach work with his team, an idea struck me. Why couldn't our family operate like a team too?

"So I went home and talked it over with Jane. Together we came up with a game plan. We noted all the household chores we could think of on a piece of paper. Then we jotted all the ones that any of us could do on a new sheet. This one we called, 'Team Chores.' The chores we didn't think the kids were ready for, or that we were nervous might cause them injury, we put on another new sheet called 'Coach's Chores.'

"That week we called a family meeting. At the meeting, Jane and I explained that a family was like a team. Each member was an important and necessary contributor. Only if everyone did their share to the best of their ability could the team be a winning one. First we asked the kids to share their thoughts on what it meant to be a winning team and what 'rewards' were earned by winning teams. They came up with things like 'they get to do what they want' and 'they're popular' and 'they have more fun.' We talked about what it could mean for us as a family to be a winning team. Through this conversation we all agreed we'd have a lot more fun working and a lot more time for playing if we were a winning team.

"Jane and I brought out the list of 'Coach's Chores.' We talked about why she and I needed to do these. Joe and Jamie were surprised to see how much we did that they never really thought about. Then we shared the list of 'Team Chores.' At first it got a big groan. Then Jane jumped in and said 'I want to do the dusting so nobody breaks anything and everything gets put back in its place' and that just started the ball rolling. Jamie grabbed doing the dishes because she liked getting them clean. Joe yelled out he wanted to mow the lawn because he liked being outside. Everyone agreed that we should all clean our own rooms.

"Whenever we got stuck, either Jane and I would

nab one chore or we would talk about who should have it based on what we are each best at. In no time, every item on the list was claimed. We made a game of it."

"Wow," was all James could utter. He thought a minute, wondering if he'd be able to pull it off with his family. "Well, no harm in trying," he finally added, "Thanks, Jones," and off he went. He needed to talk to Joyce, and fast.

James and Joyce talked over the team strategy used by the Jones family. Joyce loved the idea and was surprised it had never come up in conversations with Jane. Regardless, she was eager to try it out. They gave it a test run that week in a family meeting in much the same way as the Joneses, but with a few creative tweaks of their own. Unfortunately, the kids did not respond well at all. They sat in their chairs sullenly, displaying little to no "team spirit." After a couple of attempts from different angles, James swallowed his disappointment and asked, "What's wrong, guys?"

Jolie started to cry. "This just reminds me that I may get kicked off the soccer team because of my grades," she sobbed.

Jake was testy, "Yeah," he added, "I can't even

manage my homework as it is and you want me to do more?"

"Oops," James thought. How could he have been so blind. His heart was in the right place but he got the cart before the horse. Desperately trying to think of something to say to get out of the awkwardness of the moment, James blurted, "Coach's time out!" Joyce looked at him with eyes wide , slowly letting out the breath she had been holding.

Jake said, "Can we go now?"

Jolie added, "Yeah, can we go now? I have a big science project due on Monday."

And they both shuffled off to their rooms looking more dejected than ever.

"Oh that didn't go well at all," James said.

Joyce just shook her head.

"Don't worry, Honey," James soothed Joyce, putting his arm around her. "I think we just missed a step or two. Let me talk to Jones again. Jamie and Joe are doing great in school. I know Jake and Jolie are bright kids, so we just have to find out what's different between them."

"Okay," Joyce agreed again, "they sure looked

downcast. I hope there's something we can do. I've been feeling so helpless with all this. I try to help them with their homework, but it seems I only end up getting in their way or making them feel worse. I sure wish I knew the special language it takes to communicate with kids."

"I have an idea," James suggested. "Why don't we *both* go talk to Jones and Jane. Jones helped me so much at work. And while I know he could help me again, we're in this together. I know Jane plays a significant role in how great things are in that family. So this time let's have both of them coach both of us. What do you say?"

"Sounds like a winning idea to me."

○ 3 ○

James and Joyce Get Coached

It just so happened that one evening the next week the kids were all off together at a school event. James and Joyce made arrangements to have Jones and Jane over for dinner and a conversation about their family meeting.

"It was terrible." Joyce shared their experience at dinner. "James and I were so excited about implementing the idea you shared with us, we just assumed our kids would react the same way as yours. It really hit home how much they are struggling in school and what a huge negative impact that is having on their self-esteem. I'm worried about them and have no idea what to do about it."

"I'm so sorry," Jane replied. "I guess we did a lot with the kids in terms of their studies before trying the 'coach and team chores' thing out, and that's why it was better received. The kids were on a high because everything was going so well for them. I think they felt like they could tackle anything and succeed."

"So how did they get to that point?" Joyce asked. "I think Jake and Jolie are bright kids. I just don't understand why they're doing so poorly." Her head drooped as she blinked back tears. Jane got up from her chair and put her arm around her best friend. She could see that James had put his hand on his wife's knee.

"This is going to get better!" Jane told her adamantly. "Let Jones and I talk about some of the things we've done with Joe and Jamie. I don't think we had a plan in the beginning, we just bumbled along, but we're glad to share all our trials and tribulations and all our successes and failures. We'll just throw everything up on the wall and see what sticks."

"Yeah," Jones chimed in, then rubbed his chin.

"Hmm, where to begin. Let's think for a minute now. When did we start noticing anything different between the kids?"

"I don't think the difference between Joe and Jake dawned on me until I started seeing it between Jolie and Jamie," Joyce offered. "And as I think about it, things began changing when the kids were placed in different classes. Yes, that's it! I noticed it when Jolie and Jamie were in different classes for the first time. That was the beginning of this school year. And I remember thinking then that things had been different between Jake and Joe for a while by that time."

"Yes," Jane agreed, "I think you're right about that. Jamie has an incredible teacher this year. She has taught me so much. I guess I never realized how much until now. I think she made a huge impact on Jamie and on us." She gave Jones's hand a squeeze to emphasize her point.

"Oh, yes," Jones added. "She is amazing. And you know what? Joe also had her for a teacher in the sixth grade, and that's when Joe and Jake started to be in different classes. Jake had another teacher that year. I think we're onto something here."

"So what's so incredible about this teacher?" James chimed in.

"Well," Jane began, "her name is Mrs. Edwards." The first thing I noticed about her is her absolute love for the kids. I mean, it's genuine. She loves her job, and she really seems to understand the kids. She is also amazingly patient."

"The patience of a saint," Jones muttered, nodding his head.

"Okay, so she loves the kids," Joyce said growing impatient for something she could hold onto. "But what does she *do* that's so different?"

"The thing that really jumped out for me," Jane said, "is she explains assignments and expectations very clearly to her students. She describes in detail all the requirements of the assignment—what has to be a certain way and where they have some creative freedom. She even writes the assignments out along with the expectations and point values associated with the expectations. Then she asks them to repeat back what she said, so she knows they understood the information."

"Yes," Jones jumped in, "and in our parent-teacher conference she explained this idea of clarifying expectations and asking the children to paraphrase what they heard as a way we could help them with their homework in addition to what she does in the classroom. In this way the teacher and parents are partners in helping the kids learn. We put it to the test at home and it really worked. I remember thinking how ironic it was that I used very similar strategies when delegating to my staff at work, but I never thought of using it at home with my kids."

Jane nodded in agreement, then added, "What surprised me was how many times the kids previously had homework assignments they were very unclear about. And their grades suffered as a result. They never asked the teacher for clarification about their assignments in class. They told me they didn't want to appear stupid in front of the other kids or they just never thought about it at all."

"Hmm," James muttered, "very interesting." He was feeling quite excited. This was exactly what Jones had taught him at work as the second step in the delegation process. He mastered it at work so he felt certain he could master it at home too.

"I hate to stop here," Jane said, looking at her watch. "But the kids will be home any minute. We'd better get going. Thank you so much for dinner."

"No," Joyce said, "Thank you! This was very helpful. If you can think of anything else you learned from Mrs. Edwards, we'd appreciate hearing it. In the meantime, we'll try this technique on for size."

After the Joneses left, Joyce grabbed James's hand. "It sounds so simple; almost too simple. What do you think?"

"It was the same coaching as the second step in the delegation process Jones taught me at work. I know it was effective there. I can only imagine it will work at home too. I'm sure ready to try. We're out of other ideas, so let's give it a shot. We certainly don't have anything to lose."

The next night after dinner, Joyce and James joined the kids when they went to their rooms to start their homework assignments. James went with Jake and Joyce with Jolie.

"So what assignments do you have tonight, Jolie?" Joyce inquired.

"Oh, science, of course," Jolie rolled her eyes. She

didn't like science much. "And math and English."

"Which one are you going to tackle first?"

"Math," it was Jolie's favorite subject.

"Can you tell me what your assignment is?"

"Sure, but it's really easy. Science is the one that will be hard."

"Okay, what's the science assignment?"

"Well, we're supposed to research and compare the dinosaurs of the different eras."

"Jolie, I'm surprised at you. You love dinosaurs! Why is this such a tough assignment?"

"Because," Jolie moaned, "I never really know what the teacher is looking for. Every time I think I understand and have the assignment right, I end up getting a bad grade. I don't get it!" She stomped her foot in conclusion, expressing her frustration.

Despite the scowl on Jolie's face, Joyce felt ecstatic. They were onto something. "What did the teacher tell you, *exactly?*"

As Jolie described the assignment as precisely as she could, a couple of things became clear to Joyce. First, Joyce realized she didn't understand the assignment either and second, she realized there were things both Jolie and the teacher could do to make it more clear. "Okay, Jolie," Joyce began, "let's talk about what you can do to better understand your assignments. That way you'll know what to do and you'll get better grades."

"Will it help me stay on the soccer team?"

"I believe so. Do you want to give it a try?"

Jolie nodded, a bit of skepticism slipping out. But Joyce was undaunted. She walked Jolie through what Jones and Jane had shared with her the night before. When she was finished, Jolie wrote the information on the front of her notebook so she wouldn't forget.

"So, you'll do that tomorrow with your science assignment, right?" Joyce asked her.

"Yes," Jolie answered, "and my English assignment too, because I don't get that one either!"

After looking the English assignment over with Jolie, Joyce realized that, as with the science assignment, she wasn't clear what was expected either. But, although she couldn't help her with the content of the assignment, she knew she helped a great deal with the process of getting assignments done correctly. And that was most important. She breathed a sigh of relief as she quietly walked out of Jolie's room. Jolie glanced at her just before she shut the door.

"Thanks, mom," she said quietly.

"You're welcome, Sweetie."

Later that night Joyce and James compared notes. James's experience with Jake went much the same way. They were surprised that the frustration and failure both kids were experiencing in school could be boiled down to something so easy.

"Knowing Jones," James chuckled, "we've just uncovered the tip of the iceberg. At least that was my experience with him at work. But I think we're making progress and that is what's important."

"Good point!" she exclaimed and grabbed a small notebook she kept on the nightstand.

"What are you doing?" James asked.

"I'm taking an idea from Jolie. She wrote what I told her in her notebook so she wouldn't forget. Since you say there is more we'll be learning from Jane and Jones, I want to take notes so I don't forget."

"Right." James agreed. "That's what I did at the

office too. I wrote notes on my whiteboard. That was very helpful."

"So is it okay in this notebook? We can both refer to it."

"Sure, that will work."

This is what Joyce wrote:

When giving kids a task, be very specific about what is expected. Ask them to repeat it back to make sure they understood. Help them learn how to get this same clarification with their assignments in school.

Joyce thought for a minute, "Hmmm, I wonder," she murmured.

"What?" James inquired.

"Well, I think there might be another step before this one."

"Really? What are you thinking?"

"Well," Joyce explained, "We kind of jumped headlong into things with the kids and it didn't turn out very well. I think if we had spent more time thinking about what we were trying to accomplish we would have had a better result. We could have been better prepared. Yes, that's it," she said picking up the notebook and pen again.

"What's it?" James asked.

She turned her notebook so he could read it:

Prepare in advance.

"That should be the first step," Joyce added.

"I believe you're right, Joyce, much as I hate to admit it when you're right," Jones teased.

Joyce gave him a playful punch, "Yes, and it's too bad you have to admit it so often," she teased back.

The rest of that week, the kids came home each night filled with excitement because they better understood their homework. After dinner each evening they ran up to their rooms to get their assignments done. It was clear their confidence in being able to complete the assignments correctly was increasing. All in all, it was a happier week in the James household than they'd had in a while. The kids even had some spare time after their homework to play outside. All of them enjoyed that new development.

4

Time for Step Three

Eager to share their exciting developments, the Jameses decided to have the Joneses over for dinner every two weeks. The kids all attended a school event together twice a month, so it was a perfect time to meet. This gave them the opportunity to not only talk about how things went during the previous two weeks but to learn what they needed to tackle the next two weeks and to have enough time to practice the new skills.

"So, how did it go?" Jones asked as he walked in the door behind his wife. He seemed as eager to hear the news as James and Joyce were to share it.

"Yes, do tell," Jane said.

"So far, so good," James answered, taking their coats. "We showed them how to be sure they understood their assignments and how to ask for clarification when they didn't and they picked up on it right away. They seemed delighted to get some help and things have improved considerably. There still is a ways to go though."

"How's that?" Jane inquired.

"Well it seems the kids are getting better at doing the assignments correctly, but they're not very good at getting them done on time," Joyce explained. "They just don't seem to be able to manage their time very well or to predict how long something will take. James and I have talked about it, but we're not sure how to help them. Do you have any suggestions?"

Jane and Jones exchanged glances and smiled. It looked like they were sharing a moment remembered. Just as James was about to ask them what they were thinking, Jane began, "We encountered that too. I had almost forgotten about it, it seems so long ago now."

"What seems so long ago?" Joyce asked with a hint of impatience. She wanted to learn this stuff and get the kids back on track fast.

Jane started relating the story, "It was our second parent-teacher conference with Mrs. Edwards. She told us Joe was falling behind in his studies. Of course, we already knew that. Our first scare with him was when his grades started going down. We weren't sure what the problem was because we knew he understood his assignments. We asked Mrs. Edwards what she thought was wrong. She just smiled in her patient way and assured us that what Joe was experiencing was typical of children his age. Her manner was so reassuring, it really helped us cope."

"Yes, it got us thinking more about how to help, rather than lamenting over our child 'having a problem.' She mobilized us," Jones added.

Jane continued, "She told us that the workload in school tends to increase about the same time as kids get more interested in social activities, so it becomes more difficult for them to manage their time. As parents, we can help them with this, since we've, for the most part, already learned these skills. Even if we're not great at managing our time, we usually know what we could do to better manage it and can share that information with our children."

"I have to admit," Jones chimed in again, "helping Joe through this helped me become better at time management too. I saw he had picked up a lot of my bad habits already. So if I was to help him, I had to not only teach him the skills, I had to model better habits."

Jane chuckled as she recalled the experience, "It was pretty funny when I overheard Jones telling Joe something he could do to manage his studies better, knowing Jones didn't practice what he was preaching."

"And she usually informed me of that after the fact too," Jones chuckled, giving his wife's arm an affable squeeze.

Joyce couldn't hold back. "So what did Mrs. Edwards tell you to do with Joe?"

"Oh yes," Jane said, "the most important part.

"Mrs. Edwards told us there are many ways a person can budget his time so it's important for each person to find the way that best suits him. She suggested we buy Joe a big calendar that he could put on the wall. On the calendar he could write all his assignments on their respective due dates in one color of ink. In another color of ink, he could write in his basketball practice, and his social activities in a third color. Once he had everything written on the calendar he needed to 'budget' the time it would take for each of his assignments, taking into consideration his other assignments, social activities, basketball practices, and other events he had planned. She said she did the same thing with him at school with his school assignments, and he was already improving. Using the same process at home really reinforces his learning and helps us help him too. It's pretty cool because she sometimes has students make their own calendars or gets them donated by local companies."

Jones couldn't help but jump in again. "Doing this with Joe was the point when I realized I needed to start making better use of my calendar at work. When I saw all the activities he was juggling, I couldn't help but want to better understand my own."

Jane giggled, "This was also the time we realized Joe had inherited one of Jones's worst traits."

"Hey, I resemble that remark," Jones teased.

"What trait was that, pray tell?" James eyed Jones curiously.

"Procrastination!" Jane cried out, shocked James didn't know.

"I don't think I was ever aware of that bad habit of yours, Jonsey," James said, playfully slapping his cousin on the shoulder.

Joyce couldn't help herself, "Probably because you share it." She laughed loudly with Jane joining in until they were both almost reduced to tears. The cousins merely watched them with frowns on their faces and hands on their hips.

"Are you quite done?" Jones asked emphatically, trying to move the subject off him. He cracked a smile though, welcoming humor, even at his own expense. "Let's get back to business here. We haven't much time left."

"Yes," James agreed. "So you got Joe this calendar and had him write all his assignments and activities on it in different colors of ink. Is that right?"

"Right," Jane answered. "Back to the subject of budgeting Joe's time. Mrs. Edwards suggested that once everything was on the calendar, Joe needed to estimate the time it would take him for each of his larger assignments and write in a start date that would allow him sufficient time to complete the assignment on schedule. He was then to connect the start date to the finish date with a line, meaning that he needed to work on this task over these days, and finally, he needed to note how much time per day would be spent on it. With those subjects he wasn't as fond of, or that were more difficult, Mrs. Edwards suggested he add in an extra day just to be sure he completed them on time.

"When we did this with Joe, his procrastination became obvious. We learned Joe had been doing all of his favorite assignments first, even if they didn't take very long. Then he moved on to the easiest assignments. Finally, he saved his toughest assignments for last, which was why he never completed them on time."

"Well, he had a method, it just wasn't a very good one," Jones chuckled. "So we were able to help him develop a better one, thanks to Mrs. Edwards. And I have to admit, I've used it at the office too. It really does work."

"Okay, so I think we're set for our next step with the kids. What do you think, Joyce? Are you ready?" James put an arm around his wife.

"Ready?" Joyce exclaimed, "I can't wait!"

Jones and Jane strolled home together, arm in

arm. It was a pleasant night, balmy with a full moon lighting their way.

"This is fun, helping them out and reinforcing what we learned at the same time," Jones said as he pulled Jane closer.

"Yes, it is," Jane agreed. "I'm glad we can help."

Meanwhile, Joyce and James were feeling much more relaxed and hopeful than they were before dinner. They cleaned up the dishes and sat for a moment on the couch in the family room.

"Let's do this with the kids together this time," Joyce broke into the lazy quiet between them. "I think it will work better than each of us trying to help them individually. What do you think?"

"I think it's a great idea. You're the best, Joyce. I know it probably sounds mushy but working this through with you, with all of us as a family, I feel closer to you than ever. And that's pretty close."

Joyce smiled at James, then leaned her head on his shoulders. She couldn't have agreed more.

The next day, Joyce ran out on her lunch hour to pick up some big calendars for the kids. She was close to a bookstore, so it was easy to zip in and out with plenty of time left to eat a bite. She chose a calendar with cats on it for Jolie. Jolie loved cats, so Joyce knew she would be excited to have it, and better yet, use it. For Jake she picked out a calendar of Spiderman. He was a big fan of Spiderman, and Joyce thought the superhero would encourage Jake to be more successful. He needed all the help he could get because, like James, Jones, and Joe, he was a procrastinator. "What was it with these men, anyway?" she giggled to herself.

Joyce wrapped their calendars in fun paper and that night at dinner the kids were presented with their gifts. "Wow, Spiderman! Cool!" Jake hollered as he ripped off the wrapping paper.

"Kitties!" Jolie squealed in delight once she got hers open.

"But, Mom," Jake looked from Joyce to James quizzically, "why did you buy us calendars? That's weird!"

"Yeah, weird!" Jolie echoed.

James jumped in, "The calendars are from both of us to both of you. We're going to show you how to use them to help you do better in school. Come on, let's head into the family room and your mom and I will explain."

Joyce and James took turns explaining what they were going to do and why. Joyce had also purchased colored markers and asked the kids to pick out several of the colors they wanted to use to write all the information on their calendars. They had quite a fun time reminding each other of various practices, social activities, and appointments. The kids ran upstairs to get their homework assignments so they would know what to write and on what date. By the time they finished, it was bedtime.

Jolie carried her calendar up to her room looking it all over. She almost banged into the door; she was so captivated with it. She placed it prominently on one wall above her little desk.

Jake had charged up the stairs to his room before Jolie could hit the first step. James and Joyce knew it was a hit when he took down one of his favorite Spiderman pictures and put the calendar in its place.

James checked in with the kids one last time before heading to bed himself. As they got ready for bed, James asked Joyce, "How do you think we did?"

"I think it went amazingly well."

"Me too," James said as a big smile spread across his face. "Now we just have to make sure they use them and keep them updated."

Joyce chuckled, "I guess we'll just have to put that on our calendar."

Before they called it a night, Joyce grabbed her notebook off the nightstand. This is what she wrote:

Buy calendars and have the kids write their assignments, practices, and extracurricular activities on the calendar in different colors of ink. For larger assignments, have them estimate the time required and write in a start date as well as a due date. Then have them draw a line between the two dates indicating that this assignment has to be worked on over these days. Finally, have them note how much time will be allotted to this assignment each day. Make sure they keep the calendar up to date.

○ **5** ○

James and Joyce Define Authority

At their next dinner, James and Joyce were excited to share their news of how well the kids responded to their calendars. During the previous two weeks, they had walked the kids to their rooms after dinner each night to look at the calendars and make sure they were working on the assignments they had written out. They also worked with them to make sure new information was added to the calendars. By the end of the two weeks, Jake and Jolie were both able to actively use and update the calendars on their own. They both had also received good feedback from their teachers about getting their assignments in on time.

But while all went well on timing, they ran into another unexpected glitch. And this is what they wanted to discuss with Jones and Jane at dinner. The "glitch" happened at home, but James and Joyce could imagine it happening at school too, so they wanted to check to see if Jones and Jane could share any useful tips or had any similar experiences.

"Hey, ya' all!" Jones hollered as he peeked his head in the front door, "We're here for our feeding!"

"C'mon in," Joyce called, "we're in the kitchen."

Jane came in the kitchen first and gave James and Joyce each a hug. "Mmm, smells good. What are we having?"

"Fettuccine Alfredo," Joyce said, "Your favorite."

"There goes my diet," Jane exclaimed. "And yours too," she added, poking Jones in the stomach.

"What diet?" Jones joked, "My philosophy is 'Eat today, diet tomorrow, and tomorrow never comes.'"

"Well, we know you'll be running it off tomorrow morning at the crack of dawn, so go ahead and indulge tonight," James said as he finished setting the table. "Have a seat."

"So how did everything go?" Jane asked, anxious to hear.

"Great!" James and Joyce said in unison.

"Well at least the calendar project went well, and so did things with school," Joyce added. "But we encountered a hiccup with something at home and hoped you would have some thoughts about it."

"Oh?" Jane asked, curious, "What happened?"

"James, why don't you tell them while I dish up here?" Joyce asked.

"Be glad to. Let's see. It was over the weekend. Kind of a funny story really," James chuckled. "We went to the grocery store and left the kids home to clean up the breakfast dishes. We didn't think we were gone that long, but when we came home we were shocked to find all the dishes, including the good china, out on the countertop."

"Oh?" Jane said raising an eyebrow, "What was that all about?"

"Well, bless their hearts," Joyce continued, "It seemed they were so excited about how much we had helped them with their study problems and were feeling so much better about how they were doing that they wanted to surprise us by doing something special. So they decided to take the 'clean-up-the-kitchen' request a bit further. They decided to clean out all the cupboards and rearrange them!"

"Oh my gosh!" Jane exclaimed with wide eyes as she burst into laughter. "What did you do?"

"Well, we thanked them very much for their thoughtfulness but let them know that the cupboards were arranged the way they were for a reason, and if everything was moved around it would be difficult to find things. It would make dinner preparations and clean-up a lot harder. I felt badly though, because it seemed they were deflated as a result. Here they had tried to extend such a nice gesture and it didn't work out well at all."

Jones chuckled to himself, shaking his head.

"What?" James asked, "What are you thinking?"

"Well, we had a similar thing occur only it was with Jamie at school. Apparently she was doing so well in science after having struggled with it for some time that the science teacher wanted to reward her with some extra responsibility and recognition. She was beaming with pride when she first told us. Several weeks later, however, Jamie came home so dejected it almost broke our hearts."

"Oh yes," Jane jumped in, recalling the incident, "The turtle tale!"

"The turtle tale?" Joyce asked inquisitively.

"If you'll let me finish," Jones joked and continued with the story. "So Jamie got the responsibility of feeding the class turtle after school each day. She was so proud and excited when the teacher first gave it to her that it was hard to imagine anything going wrong with something so simple. But kids will be kids. Anyway, she thought if being helpful was so much fun, why not be more helpful and surprise the teacher, much like your Jake and Jolie wanted to surprise you."

"What did she do?" James queried. "Well, without asking or telling anyone, she started feeding the guppies in the fish tank in addition to the turtle. What she didn't know was that another student fed them in the morning. After about a week, some of the fish died and were floating around the top of the tank when the kids came to school. It was quite a scene with some of the kids crying about the dead fish. By the next day more fish had died. The teacher was a bit dismayed as to why so many were suddenly dying. He was talking to the class about what causes fish to die, trying to settle them down and happened to mention that they can die from overfeeding. Jamie piped up, saying, 'But I didn't overfeed them!' It all came out then that she was feeding them as well as the student who fed them in the morning. You can imagine how devastated and upset she was that she killed the fish and had half the class and the teacher upset with her, when all she was trying to do was to be helpful."

"Oh that's a horrible story!" Joyce exclaimed. "Poor Jamie. What did you do to console her?"

"Well, her science teacher wasn't much help since he was upset, even though he understood. We managed to help her get through the emotion of it. But what we really wanted was to keep something like that from happening again. And we knew we needed help with that. So we called Mrs. Edwards. Of course, she had some great words of wisdom. She told us that with any task or chore we assign to children we should carefully outline the limits of their responsibility and authority. Meaning that they should do no more than, and no less than, what we are asking and explain why this is important. She told us she learned this lesson the hard way with her teenage son. Apparently she allowed him use of the family car one evening to go to a movie with some friends. Several hours later she got a call from her son that they were in a town fifty miles away with a flat tire. You can imagine how upset she and her husband were that the boys decided to go joy-riding rather than see the movie. From then on she said she always clarified the boundaries of his responsibility and his authority to make decisions. She said that was a valuable lesson she learned for the classroom also, and she's now very careful to be clear on both when giving a task to a student. Just as she puts her assignments in writing, she often puts this in writing too."

"Wow," James muttered. "This topic sure gives one pause. It seems we were all lucky that nothing more serious happened. I guess we should count our blessings and be sure our kids understand their limits from now on."

"Yup, that's what we took from it too," Jones agreed, "although sometimes it's hard to think of all the potential pitfalls in advance. So you really have to take time to explain things to the kids and to coax them to talk about what they are hearing and understanding so you make sure you both understand what should happen and what *could* happen. It's more time-consuming, but only in the short run. In the long run, it avoids some of the problems we've talked about."

"So let me be sure I have this right," Joyce said, "We should outline the limits of their authority—their responsibility and freedom—when we give them a task to do, right?"

"Yes," Jane jumped in. "And I would also encourage you to talk with them in depth about what they understand they can and cannot do from what you've said. A good way to do that is to ask the kids to paraphrase what you said. This gives you a chance to catch anything that may have been unclear or missed.

"Another thing we did was give the kids some ideas about what they could do to surprise or help us, if and when they wanted to. That way, we would find it truly helpful and it would be a surprise, since we didn't know when, or if, they would do any of the things on that list."

"Oh, that's a great idea," Joyce exclaimed. "I like that."

"Well, I'm afraid it's about that time," Jones said, consulting his watch.

"Oh, yes, it has gotten late," Jane agreed. "We'd better head out. Good luck with things this week!'

The very next night an opportunity arose for James and Joyce to test their new skills. Jake had basketball practice immediately after school. Some of the boys in practice, along with Jake, were planning to grab a bite to eat after practice, then head back to school to work on the upcoming school play. Jake's grades had improved to the point where he could once again be involved in after-school activities, so he had joined the set crew for the play. The boys wanted to work on the set for a few hours, then go to Jeff's house to listen to some new CDs he got as a birthday gift. As Jake announced his plans to his parents, James and Joyce knew they were going to have to step in.

"Okay, let me make sure I heard you right. You want to go to basketball practice, then grab a bite to eat, then go back to school to work on the set for the play, then got to Jeff's house to listen to CDs, right? That sounds like an awful lot of activity for a school night, Jake," James began.

"It's cool," Jake responded quickly.

"It sounds cool," Joyce jumped in, "but let's consult your calendar just to make sure nothing is falling through the cracks."

Jake dejectedly trudged up the stairs to his room with his parents following.

"Let's see," James traced his finger along the calendar to the current week. "Looks like you have a project due tomorrow that you've been working on each day. Is that right?"

"Yes," Jake agreed, "And it's going great. I'm almost done."

"So, have you done the work on it today in order to finish it by tomorrow?" James inquired.

"No," Jake said softly, with his head drooping perceptibly.

"When did you plan to work on it today?" Joyce asked encouragingly.

"Tonight," Jake said sullenly.

"When tonight?" Joyce pushed.

"I don't know; when I have the time."

"Well, son," James explained, "it seems like you won't have the time if you do all the activities you said you wanted to do tonight. So what is more important to you? To do these activities tonight or to get your assignment in on time so you can continue to do activities in the future?"

"I wish I didn't have to choose. It's hard. I want to be with my friends too."

"I know, son," James put an arm on his son's shoulder. "How about a compromise? How about if you go to practice, get a bite to eat, go do the work on the play, and then come home and do your homework? That way you get some time with your friends and get your homework done too."

"I guess," Jake said, not wanting to let go of his plans.

"It's your choice, but you also have to live with the consequences."

"Okay," Jake finally agreed, "That's what I'll do then."

"So, tell us what you're going to do so we're clear," Joyce asked, remembering what she learned about asking the kids to paraphrase what they heard to make sure they understand.

"I'm going to go to basketball practice right after

school, then get a bite to eat, then go back to school to work on the set for awhile, then come home and do my assignment."

"Good," James said encouragingly. "So how long is practice?"

"Fifty minutes."

"And where are you going to eat?"

"McDonald's"

"What time will you be back to school to work on the set?"

"Well, let's see," Jake said counting on his fingers. "4:00 to 5:00 is practice, 5:00 to 5:30 to eat, so we should be back at the school about 5:30."

"Then how long do you plan on working on the set? How much time do you need for your homework?"

"Probably two hours for my homework so I guess I'd better leave school around 7:30."

"How about *by* 7:30?"

"Okay."

"Okay," James summarized, "practice for an hour, McDonald's for one half hour, set work on the play for two hours, and home no later than 7:45, right? No other plans, no other distractions, right?"

"Yes, sir!" Jake said, mocking a military response, snapping his hand at an angle to his eyebrow, but cracking a smile too.

"At ease, soldier," James joined in the joke.

"Oh, dad," Jake groaned. "Can I go now that you're done drilling me?"

"Yes, you can go now that I'm done drilling you, but I reserve the right to drill you again in the future."

Joyce grabbed Jake for a hug on his way out.

After he left, James let out a long, slow breath. "How'd we do?"

"We were great," Joyce reassured him. "That last part, 'No other plans, no other distractions, right?' was right out of our last 'lesson' with the Joneses: defining the limits of his authority. Well done. I would have forgotten that."

"Maybe, but you remembered the paraphrasing I had forgotten."

"We make a good team then," Joyce laughed.

"Yes, we do."

That night as they got ready for bed, Joyce grabbed her trusty notebook. In it she wrote:

Clearly outline the limits of their authority. Make sure they understand the boundaries of their responsibility and freedom. Be specific. Ask them to paraphrase what they heard to make sure they understand. Have them list what they will and won't do or can and can't do to make sure all bases are covered.

They spent the next fifteen minutes brainstorming ideas about what the kids could do to surprise them. They created a fairly good list. When the ideas started to get corny and extravagant, they knew it was time to get some shut-eye. "Let's review it tomorrow and give it to them this weekend," Joyce said. But as she turned to see if James agreed she saw he was already starting to snore. She kissed his cheek and spooned with him. She was feeling more relaxed and happy than she had in a while. Things seemed right in her world again.

∘ 6 ∘

Operation Checkpoint

The next two weeks went by quickly. Nothing much new came up to struggle with—Joyce and James were beginning to think they would have a dinner without a lesson for a change. Maybe they had learned as much as they needed to know. The kids were doing much better in school and both were fully back into their after-school activities.

That's what they were thinking until that afternoon when Jolie came home in tears. She had turned in her biggest project of the year the previous week and got it back that day with a poor grade. She was devastated. After all her hard work, she couldn't understand why she had done so poorly.

"Come here, Jolie," Joyce said soothingly to her daughter. She pulled her up on her lap, and Jolie rested her head on her mother's shoulders. Joyce could feel her daughter's tears drop onto her neck and it almost broke her heart. She took a deep breath and began, "I'm so sorry this happened, Jolie." She gave her daughter a hug. "Do you want to see if we can figure out what went wrong?"

"I guess," Jolie sobbed.

Joyce silently reviewed the steps she had learned so far to see if she could find some answers.

"Let's see, did you understand the assignment, Honey?"

"I thought I did! I asked the teacher to clarify it when she gave it to us, and I repeated back what I heard. She said I was right."

"Okay, did you turn it in on time?"

"Yes, I did. Since it was such a big project I wrote it on my calendar extra early. I worked on it every day for over a week. I was actually done with it a day early, so I used the last day to read it over to make sure it was all correct."

"That sounds really good, Jolie. Good job!"

"No, it wasn't!" she cried, "I got a C-minus for all my hard work. That's hardly a *good job*!"

"Well, let's look at your paper to see what your teacher wrote about your grade."

Jolie pulled her project out of her backpack. She turned it to the last page where her teacher had made comments. This is what was written there:

"Jolie, I'm not sure how you got this far off track with your assignment. We talked about it when I first assigned it and it seemed you understood what was required, but somewhere you got off track. While this is an interesting study, it is not what the assignment required."

"Curious," was all Joyce could think to say. "Do you have any idea of where you got off track, Jolie?"

"No," Jolie said quietly with her head hanging and her lower lip protruding. She was not a happy little girl.

"Tell you what," Joyce said. "Let's both think about this for a while. Then let's talk about it tomorrow and maybe with a fresh perspective we can figure out what went wrong, okay?"

"Okay." Jolie slid off her mother's lap and went straight to her room, shutting the door behind her. For Jolie, that was a sign she was truly upset.

"Whew!" Joyce sighed after Jolie left the room. She had bought some time. Hopefully Jones and Jane would have an answer to this one, because she was stumped.

That night, Joyce explained what happened to Jones and Jane over dinner. She shared how deflated Jolie had been and how at a loss she felt to help her. "Any ideas?" she asked.

"As a matter of fact," Jane spoke up, "we have."

"Thank goodness, let's have it!"

"Joe encountered a similar problem with a project he had for school a year ago. He clarified the assignment with the teacher and paraphrased what he heard. He used his calendar to set the timeline and worked on it diligently every day. He turned it in on time and was convinced he would get an A on it. Unfortunately, when he got it back with a C, he was very upset. We talked about it when he got home, but we were both puzzled as to what went wrong. Jones got involved then too, remember Honey?"

"Yes, I do remember. I'm afraid I wasn't much help either."

"What did you do?" Joyce asked, curious what they came up with.

"Well, by now you can probably guess," Jane said with a giggle. "I called Mrs. Edwards."

"We're going to have to meet her one of these days." James said.

"Yes," Joyce agreed, "But for now, let's just hear how she helped with this dilemma."

"She was not surprised that Joe's grade suffered even though he theoretically understood the assignment and used his calendar to complete it on time. She told us that with protracted assignments, it is easy for kids to get off track, even if they clearly understood the assignment in the beginning. Many times they get engrossed in some detail on the one hand, or get off on a tangent on the other hand, depending on the individual.

"She told us it is extremely important to set checkpoints with them to ensure they are progressing along with the task as they should. By periodically checking in on their progress, it is easy to catch them before they get too far into a detail or too far off on a tangent and bring them back on track. She said the longer the task is drawn out, the more checkpoints should be set. She also said it would be good to set them close together at first, then, as you see they're doing okay they can be set further apart.

"She does this with extended projects in the classroom too; checking in with the entire class at given points along the way to make sure they're staying on track. She explained that because she allows students to earn points for the drafts they turn in at these checkpoints along the way, students who are struggling with the project are helped because they get feedback and earn points throughout the process, rather than just at the end. She said it also helps prevent good students from just slapping something together at the last minute and, therefore, not really learning from the exercise. Finally, checkpoints help with those who may not be using their calanders and time lines effectively.

"She said the students ultimately do better with this approach. Since she suggested we use it at home, Joe and Jamie have been doing much better."

"This is sounding awfully familiar," James said,

eyeing Jones. "This sounds similar to how you coached me with delegating at work. Did you steal Mrs. Edwards' ideas?"

Jones chuckled, "Actually no, I had thought of them all on my own. But Mrs. Edwards and the two of us were also amazed at the parallels between delegating a task or project at work and helping the kids with their assignments at school and at home. It isn't surprising that there are similarities, if you think about it. We talked about these with Mrs. Edwards and were curious and delighted about the overlap. It certainly made it easier for me to apply the skills at home, given that I used them everyday at work. I think Mrs. Edwards learned a few things from us too. We've put our heads together on challenges frequently since that discovery."

"Getting back to the point," Joyce interrupted, "James, does this mean you know what we should do to help Jolie understand where she went wrong with this assignment?"

"Well, I know how to make sure she doesn't go down the wrong path with future assignments. I use the checkpoint concept regularly at work now. As far as this assignment goes, I'm sure we'll be able to figure it out with Jolie by backtracking and asking questions to see where she either got too engrossed in some detail or got off on a tangent somehow. Knowing Jolie, I'll bet it's the former. That kid is so detail oriented, she scares me sometimes!"

"Unlike her father who tends to be quite tangential," Joyce teased.

"And just like her mother who is the queen of detail," James teased back.

"Well, regardless of who takes after whom and which tendency is better or worse, it seems you two know what to do with Jolie, am I right?" Jane broke in.

"Right," James and Joyce both agreed.

The next night Joyce caught up with Jolie after school. "Jolie," Joyce started, "I think I have some ideas about the project you got back yesterday. Do you want to discuss it?"

"I guess," Jolie responded. While she had come home from school in a jovial mood, the assignment obviously remained a sore spot.

"Can you tell me exactly what your assignment was?"

"Sure, it was for geography. We were supposed to pick a continent, other than North America or Antarctica, and choose three countries we wanted to travel to on that continent. We were supposed to say why we wanted to travel there and what the benefits and risks of traveling there might be."

"Well that sounds clear enough and like a pretty interesting assignment. So what continent and countries did you choose?"

"I chose the continent of Africa and the countries of Namibia, Kenya, and Tanzania."

"Interesting! Why did you choose them?"

"Mom!" Jolie scolded, thinking her mother should already know the answer, "because of the big cats!"

"Oh, of course," Joyce remembered, "silly me. How could I forget your cats?"

"Well, so far so good. What did you write about the benefits and risks of traveling there?"

"I guess I didn't really write about that part."

"You didn't? What do you mean? What did you write about?"

"Well, I started writing about the research that is

being done on the big cats there. You know, the cheetahs, lions, and leopards? I wrote about how they are endangered because the people are turning the places they live into farmland and then shooting them when they hunt their farm animals. But the kitties have to eat too, and the farmers are taking away their homes. It's so bad, Mom. Cheetahs are suffering the most, because they are not as strong as the other cats. Lions will even hunt cheetah, did you know that? It makes me sad. I want to go there to see if I can learn more and help somehow."

Joyce could see her daughter's passion about the "kitties" and felt for her. But she also was beginning to understand what went wrong with Jolie's assignment. "Jolie," she began softly, "Do you think you wrote more about the kitties than why you chose those countries and what the benefits and risks of traveling there would be?"

"Maybe," Jolie conceded just a little, "but the kitties were more important."

"Well, I can understand that the kitties were more important to you, but can you understand that the kitties and what is happening to them was not what the assignment called for?"

"I guess," Jolie conceded a little more.

"So the reason you got a lower grade than you wanted was because you got too focused on the detail of the kitties and overlooked the bigger picture of what the assignment required?"

"I guess so."

"I have an idea about how we can help you to make sure this doesn't happen with future assignments. Do you want to hear it?"

"Yeah, I guess," Jolie was having a hard time accepting that her treatise on kitties wasn't important enough to get a better grade.

"You sure?" Joyce tested. She knew Jolie well enough to know that until she was ready to listen, anything she said would go in one ear and out the other.

Jolie stared at her feet and dug her toe into the floor. This was her indicator that she was contemplating her next step. Joyce waited patiently.

"Okay, Mom," she said finally, "I'm ready."

"Okay. In the future, let your dad or me know when you have a big assignment. We will work with you to make sure you stay on track with it by setting checkpoints on your calendar. At the checkpoint, we'll review the assignment with you and what you've done on it so far. That way, if you're getting into too much detail or getting off on a tangent, we'll catch it and correct it early on, before you turn it in for a grade. Do you understand?"

"I think so. You mean kind of like progress reports, huh?"

"Exactly."

"But Mom?" Jolie asked. "What's a tangent?"

Joyce chuckled, "Well you know how your dad starts talking on one subject and before you know it he's moved onto others, so you lose track of what he's talking about sometimes?"

Jolie nodded and rolled her eyes. They all knew this quality of James very well.

"*That* is a tangent."

Jolie laughed and gave her mom a hug. "I don't think I go on tangents much, Mom. But Jake does!"

Joyce laughed too. "Yes, I'm afraid he inherited that from his father. But you, my dear, inherited your tendency to get too far into the details, like you did on this paper, from me. Sorry about that! But at least we know what to do about it now, right?"

"Right. Thanks, Mom."

"You're very welcome, Sweetheart."

That night Joyce shared her story with James who was all ears to hear how it went. Unfortunately he'd had a meeting and couldn't be there to share in the experience.

"Sounds like it went very well. Congratulations!" he said when she finished.

"Yes, I feel good about it. But more important, I think Jolie feels good about it. I think she understands where she went wrong, and we have a good plan to make sure it doesn't happen again."

"That's what it takes," James said. "Good for you both!"

Joyce picked up her notebook and wrote:

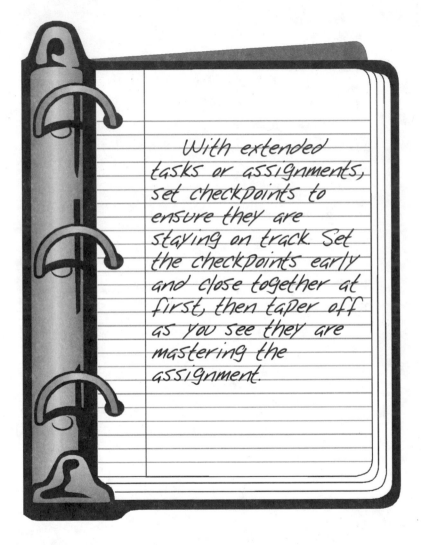

With extended tasks or assignments, set checkpoints to ensure they are staying on track. Set the checkpoints early and close together at first, then taper off as you see they are mastering the assignment.

With a big sigh of relief, she rolled over and fell immediately asleep.

∘ **7** ∘

The Wrap-Up

"Smooth sailing" would have been the words to describe the James household the next two weeks. The family, and especially the kids, seemed to have discovered a rhythm, a flow, and it felt really good. The kids were taking more and more initiative, and they were successful. They felt better about themselves, and the family was closer than they ever remembered. They had developed a tight bond, knowing that they could all depend on one another for help whenever they needed it and knowing that the help would truly be beneficial.

At their next biweekly dinner, James and Joyce

made special preparations and had purchased a gift for the Joneses. They were so appreciative, they wanted to celebrate and express their gratitude. They weren't sure whether or not they were done with all they had to learn, but they were ready to celebrate anyway. What they didn't know was that the Joneses had a surprise of their own.

When the doorbell rang, James thought something was fishy. Jones typically just came right in. "Unless it isn't Jones," he muttered to himself, growing irritated thinking it was probably somebody selling something. He opened the door and was befuddled to see it was Jane and Jones standing there. Then he saw a woman behind them. She was very petite with the thickest head of long dark curls he had ever seen. But even more startling than her hair, were her eyes. As Jones introduced her to James, her eyes twinkled and her smile made James feel instantly at ease. He knew who she was before Jones even said her name.

"*This,*" Jones said emphatically, "is Mrs. Edwards. I hope you don't mind that I invited her. I know Joyce always makes a ton of food, and I thought you two would like to meet her. She had a rare evening free, so here she is."

"Oh my gosh!" James exclaimed, closing his mouth as he realized it had been hanging open for some time. "Mrs. Edwards, it is such an honor to meet you."

"Joyce!" he yelled, as he invited the three of them in. "You have to see who's here!"

Joyce came out of the kitchen rubbing her hands on a towel. "What do you mean…" she started to say but stopped when she saw there was a newcomer to the group. "Don't tell me, let me guess. You have to be Mrs. Edwards. Am I right?"

"Right-o," Jones chuckled. "Good guess."

"It's wonderful to finally meet you! We have heard so much about you. You have helped us more than you could ever know, without even meeting us! I just want to know two things. How did you get so wise, and how can I get my kids in your classroom?"

Mrs. Edwards smiled. "It's a treat to meet you, too. Thank you for letting me pop in, as it were. It is very kind of you to be so gracious. Jane and Jones have filled me in a little on the dinners you have been having. Given how much my name seems to have come up, it's wonderful to be able to join in personally."

"Well, it seems particularly apropos this evening,

since I think it's about graduation time for us, eh Jonsey?" James asked.

"You're close," Jones teased, "I guess tonight we'll see if you made the grade, and Mrs. Edwards can be the deciding vote."

"Oh no," Mrs. Edwards said. "I don't want all that pressure! Grading in school is enough."

"Well, whether it's premature or not, we've put on the Ritz tonight," James said as he grabbed a bottle of champagne out of an ice bucket. "Jones, would you care to distribute the glasses? I'll follow you and pour. Then it's time for a toast."

"Will do," Jones agreed, grabbing the glasses off the counter and handing one to each of them.

When all the glasses were filled, James inhaled dramatically, eager to make his toast but Jones beat him to the punch, "To James and Joyce, the best ol' students ever!"

"Awh, Jones," James groaned, punching Jones playfully in the shoulder, "You *always* do that to me!"

"Well, you have to drink the toast now. You can go next."

They clinked their glasses and everyone took a sip of the bubbly.

James once again inhaled, holding up his hand forcefully in front of Jones, indicating that, by no means, should he cut him off again. With a big grin, he began, "To Jane and Jones, the best friends any couple could ever have."

Then Joyce broke in, "To Mrs. Edwards, the best teacher of all!"

"Here, here!" the cousins and their wives said in unison.

"You're too kind, but thank you," Mrs. Edwards said as she took a sip, apparently trying to hide the fact that she was blushing.

Seeing her embarrassment brought a warm chuckle from everyone. James saved her by changing the subject. He gathered the group around the table and told them they would be served Joyce's masterpiece dinner, "Roasted duck à l'orange, with her special rice pilaf and baby vegetables. And a chocolate soufflé is in the oven for dessert."

"Wow," and "Yum," were the muttered reactions, except for Jones who, in his inimitable way, hooted, "Bring it on!"

During dinner James and Joyce brought everyone

up to date on what had transpired over the last two weeks. They also filled Mrs. Edwards in on the whole story from the beginning, sharing the highlights and the tough times, what they thought they did well and what they wanted to improve on the next time. Through it all, they expressed their gratitude to her for sharing what she knew. They ended their story by saying that this dinner was a celebration of what they thought had been a very successful experience.

"It's hard to believe it's been eight weeks since we started all this," James summarized.

"In one respect it seems like it's been a long time, but when you look at all we've learned and how much things have improved, eight weeks is a short time to make things this much better," Joyce said.

"Yes," Mrs. Edwards agreed. "It seems like a long time when you're in the midst of changes. But in hindsight, it always seems like it went by fast."

"The stuff we've learned is simple and straightforward, but it really works," James said. "You can't find better tools than that."

"Absolutely," Jones chimed in. "Simple tools that really work. They sure make life a lot easier. But like all tools, they're only effective if they're used."

"Couldn't agree more," James and Joyce said, nodding in unison.

"It has really changed our lives," Joyce continued. "Seeing how these five steps can be used to help our kids be more successful is truly rewarding. But the benefit I didn't anticipate was how much it brought us closer together as a family. It's really wonderful."

Everyone remained quiet for a moment.

It was James who broke the silence. "We're so grateful to you, Jane and Jones, that we have a gift for you. If we had known you were going to be here, Mrs. Edwards, we would have had one for you too."

"To hear of your successes is gift enough for me," Mrs. Edwards replied.

"You didn't need to get us a gift," Jane said.

"We know we didn't," Joyce assured her. "We just wanted to thank you for all you've done for all of us. So this is from our family to yours." James and Joyce left the room then and came back with a large box. They had used several different kinds of paper to wrap it.

"The kids helped us pick it out and wrap it," Joyce explained.

Jones started to grab at the paper but Jane stopped him. "Wait a minute, Jones." Jane looked closely and saw that each sheet of wrapping paper was cut in a different shape. The box looked like a big beautiful collage. "This is really pretty."

"It was the kids' idea. We had a lot of fun with it."

"Okay, enough ogling the wrapping, let's open it!" Jones demanded playfully.

"Oh, Jones," Jane giggled. "You're such a big kid!"

"Well, I happen to like presents," Jones chuckled, then the smile on his face straightened.

"What is it Jones?" Jane asked.

"The wrapping paper made me think of it. It isn't five steps, it's six. We forgot one step in all this. Maybe we shouldn't celebrate yet."

"I know what's missing," James said, reading his identical cousin's mind, just like when they were kids. "A debriefing session, like the final step in the delegation process you taught me at work."

"Right," Jones nodded. "But we call it 'the wrap-up' at home."

"The wrap-up?" Joyce quizzed, "What's the wrap-up?"

"Of course! The wrap-up," Jane agreed, "I forgot about that too. Good thing you remembered, Jones. But it sounds like James is ahead of you on this one."

"Will someone please tell me what we're talking about? Am I the only one in the dark here?" Joyce inquired.

"I'm afraid so," Mrs. Edwards teased, "but I'm sure you're about to be enlightened."

"The wrap-up," James began, "is the final debriefing on what transpired. Jones taught this step to me in the delegation process at work."

"I'm still lost," Joyce muttered.

Mrs. Edwards explained, "When you have completed the first five steps, it is a good idea to have a final meeting where you talk about what everybody experienced, the high points and the low points. It helps you bring closure and learn more for the next time. It gives you a chance to talk about what went well and what could have gone better.

"It's a conversation where each person gives and receives feedback about the experience. It provides a great opportunity to confirm what you want to continue doing, what you want to improve on, and how you plan to make the improvements. And finally, it is a chance to celebrate your successes.

"I do this with each of my students at midterm and year-end. I also sometimes do it with big projects where I have worked extra closely with a student. I've even used this with parents who were very involved with their child's learning. In fact I can think of two in this very room."

Jane and Jones smiled.

Joyce brightened, "Oh, I get it! Like what we did here at dinner tonight. We talked about what we learned, what we did well, and where we still can improve. With the wrap-up, we would do that with the kids and have it be a mutual discussion, right?"

"Exactly," Mrs. Edwards exclaimed, "Good for you!"

"Beauty and brains," James said as he gave his wife a fond squeeze. "It was great going through this together. We make a terrific team."

"Yeah, yeah," Jones interrupted, "Let's cut the mush and get back to the present."

Jane socked him in the shoulder, "You're terrible! That was a sweet moment they were having."

Jones just grinned and started pulling at the wrapping. Jane joined in because she knew the opening wouldn't last long with Jones at it.

When they got it unwrapped, their jaws dropped. It was a new tent. It was huge, made out of the latest material, lightweight, waterproof, puncture-proof, with carbon fiber ultra-light tent poles, the works. James and Joyce knew the Joneses had been eyeing it for some time. Their old one was canvas and was starting to leak and tear at the seams. It was extremely heavy, so they were exhausted by the time they got it set up. They had to pray it didn't rain so their sleeping bags and clothes inside wouldn't get soaked.

Jane and Jones stared at it, then finally Jones spoke, "This is too much!"

"Not for what you did for us and for our family," Joyce said and she gave them both a big hug. James joined in on the hugs, and thank-yous were exchanged in both directions. Before Mrs. Edwards could feel too left out, James grabbed her arm and pulled her in for an enormous group hug. Everyone laughed at that.

"Time for dessert," Joyce announced as the buzzer on the oven rang.

They enjoyed their desserts over stories Mrs. Edwards shared about teaching. She told them as much as she could about how she learned all they now knew. Her wisdom and love of teaching were so evident that the Jameses and Joneses couldn't help but be in awe.

"I just wish you could teach all our kids every year," James told her, and the others nodded in agreement.

"Well, I can tell you that it is parents like you who are involved and eager to be a part of the teacher-student-parent learning team who make it not only worthwhile, but successful. It's a three-part team, and like a three-legged stool, if one leg is missing, the stool becomes very shaky. Parents are a critical part of the equation. They are the child's strongest and most stable role models. So it's what they do and say that makes the student successful or not. I only have the kids for one year. You, as parents, have them eighteen years."

"Well said," Jones agreed. "Although I know it sometimes seems like it, it's hard for me to believe there are any parents out there who don't want to help their children reach their full potential. I imagine most of them do care as much as we do, but they, like Jane and me before we learned about these steps, don't have the right tools to help their kids."

"I think that's true," said Mrs. Edwards, "That's why I try to teach this six-step program to the parents as much as I teach it to the kids. This is the best way to make the three-legged stool strong. I also share it with fellow teachers, especially my student teachers whenever I can, and then they do the same. So the word does get out.

"But, it's getting late and I still have some papers to correct. I must be heading home. Thank you so much for dinner, James and Joyce. It was so nice to meet you."

When everyone had left, James cleaned up the dinner dishes while Joyce drew a hot bath. As she soaked, she wrote the following in her notepad:

Have a wrap-up session after a large project has been completed and at the end of each week or month. Make it a discussion, giving and receiving feedback on what went well and what could be done better the next time. Agree on what improvements will be made. Celebrate successes.

She set her notepad on the edge of the tub and thought about the wrap-up sessions she and James would hold with Jake and Jolie. She was looking forward to them and thought it might be fun to get the kids some small gifts as a play on the wrap-up concept. She had started to doze when James walked in and kissed her on the forehead.

"Now don't go drowning on me," he teased her warmly. "I need my partner."

The James Gang

Joyce and James each spent time with Jake and Jolie that week doing wrap-ups of all they had been working on. It sure seemed like a different James family this weekend than it had eight short weeks ago. The wrap-ups not only went well but were very timely, as the end of the school year was fast approaching. The kids were in great spirits. Summer was just around the corner, and the last couple of months had been such a success. They were doing well in school, in their respective sports, and were enjoying after-school activities. The threats of bad grades and being removed from the teams that once hung over their heads like nasty, persistent clouds, had cleared. James and Joyce thought they seemed like different kids—cheerful, happy and secure. It was a great feeling to have come so far together.

What Jake came up with that Saturday morning at breakfast shouldn't have come as a shock, but somehow it did. James was preparing the breakfast, Jolie was setting the table, and Joyce was enjoying being waited on for a change. Jake came in rubbing the sleep out of his eyes. Since he was in charge of doing the dishes, he could afford to be a little late.

"I have a name for our team," were the first words he uttered that morning.

"Huh?" Joyce looked at him quizzically.

"What team?" asked Jolie.

"Our family team," he explained.

Everyone stopped for a minute trying to grasp what he was talking about. He looked at their blank faces and explained, "Remember a couple of months ago, you guys came to Jolie and me with lists of team chores and coaches' chores? *That* team."

"Oh!" the rest said in unison. "*That* team."

"The James Gang! I think it's a great name."

They all pondered for a minute. "I like it," James said emphatically.

"Me too!" cried Jolie excitedly, then added clarification, "only we're not outlaws or anything, right?"

"The James Gang it is," agreed Joyce. "It is a great name. Good job, Jake."

"So, can we divide up the chores today?" Jake asked. "It's close to summer, and I'd like to know what I'll be doing so I can fill in my calendar."

James and Joyce looked at each other almost stupefied. Since when did kids *ask* for a list of chores to do, they wondered.

"I know it probably sounds weird, me asking what chores I can do and all," Jake explained, reading their minds, "but you guys helped us out so much, I thought it was the least we could do." He looked at Jolie seeking her agreement.

Jolie caught the hint and added, "Yeah, it's our way of saying thanks. You gave us each a present in our wrap-ups, so this is ours to you. Besides, it's fun being on a team."

Jake walked behind Jolie, and she dropped her hand behind her back, palm up. He slapped it as he passed by, indicating his approval of her catching on.

James and Joyce looked at each other and shrugged, "Sure, why not."

So after breakfast they divided up the chores among all of them. The results were much better this time. After they finished, everyone pitched in to do the ones on their list. They were all done by noon and decided they would go to the park to play through the afternoon. And play they did.

The James Gang had become a winning team.

Help others build responsibility and self-esteem in their children. Share this book with a friend.

1. Prepare in advance.

2. When giving kids a task, be very specific about what is expected. Ask them to repeat it back to make sure they understood. Help them learn how to get this same clarification with their assignments in school as well.

3. Buy calendars and have the kids write their assignments, practices, and extracurricular activities on the calendar in different colors of ink.

For larger assignments, have them estimate the time required and write in a start date as well as a due date. Then have them draw a line between the two dates indicating that this assignment has to be worked on over these days. Finally, have them note how much time will be allotted to this assignment each day. Make sure they keep the calendar up to date.

4. Clearly outline the limits of their authority. Make sure they

understand the
boundaries of their
responsibility and
freedom. Be specific. Ask
them to paraphrase what
they heard to make sure
they understand. Have
them list what they will
and won't do or can and
can't do to make sure all
bases are covered.

5. With extended
tasks or assignments, set
checkpoints to ensure
they are staying on track.
Set the checkpoints early
and close together at

first, then taper off as you see they are mastering the assignment.

6. Have a wrap-up session after a large project has been completed and at the end of each week or month. Make it a discussion, giving and receiving feedback on what went well and what could be done better the next time. Agree on what improvements will be made. Celebrate successes.

About the Author

Psychologist Donna M. Genett has devoted the past twenty years to helping people grow personally and professionally and is an expert at helping people get things done.

Her first book, *If You Want It Done Right You Don't Have to Do It Yourself! The Power of Effective Delegation,* has been translated into thirteen languages.

Dr. Genett's "Want It Done Right" training program has helped hundreds of CEOs and other managers throughout North America to "get it done right the first time."

In this book, Dr. Genett applies her powerful principles of delegation to parenting. It's a logical segue that parents everywhere will be able to apply for the benefit of their children and themselves.

Donna Genett lives in Central California and enjoys world travel, skiing, golf, home remodeling, and competing in triathlons.

Help Your Kids Get it Done Right at Home and School!

Services and Products

Services

Speakers—Schedule a fun and powerful presentation of *Help Your Kids Get It Done Right at Home and School! Building Responsibility & Self-Esteem in Children*. Great for large groups or events.

Workshops—The *Help Your Kids Get It Done Right* training program can be delivered directly to your group. This training is an interactive workshop that takes participants deeper into the skills for building responsibility and self-esteem in children. Includes:
- four-hour workshop at your location,
- one hardcover copy of *Help Your Kids Get It Done Right at Home and School! Building Responsibility & Self-Esteem in Children*, and
- one *Help Your Kids Get It Done Right* Workbook for each participant.

Train-the-Trainer—Your trainers learn everything they need to know to conduct an impactful training of *Help Your Kids Get It Done Right at Home and School! Building Responsibility & Self-Esteem in Children*. Trainers will not only learn the skills themselves but will also learn to deliver a powerful training experience. This participative certification includes all presenter materials as well as workshop materials to train 10 participants:
- one *Help Your Kids Get It Done Right* Presenter's Guide
- one *Help Your Kids Get It Done Right* PowerPoint Presentation CD
- 11 *Help Your Kids Get It Done Right* Workbooks (10 for participants; one for trainer)
- 11 hardcover books of *Help Your Kids Get It Done Right at Home and School! Building Responsibility & Self-Esteem in Children*.

Products

***Help Your Kids Get It Done Right* Presenter's Kit**—The program to help people in organizations train their people. Includes: one PowerPoint Presentation on CD, one Presenter's Guide, 11 hardcover copies of *Help Your Kids Get It Done Right at Home and School!* , and 11 Workbooks.

***Help Your Kids Get It Done Right* Presenter's Guide**—The comprehensive guide for presenters to ensure a successful training program of *Help Your Kids Get It Done Right at Home and School!*

***Help Your Kids Get It Done Right* CD**—The PowerPoint Presentation of 75 slides used to conduct the *Help Your Kids Get It Done Right at Home and School!* training. (Can be used as a slide show or to print overheads.)

***Help Your Kids Get It Done Right* Workbook**—This 36-page workbook, used in our training programs is great for individuals wanting to learn even more.

For information about products and services, please visit
www.WantItDoneRight.com
Or call: (559) 875-7884

Help others fulfill their children's potential
for success and happiness.

To order individual copies of this book, please telephone
Quill Driver Books at 1-800-497-4909 or go to
www.QuillDriverBooks.com.

Please call Quill Driver Books Special Markets for details on
bulk quantity purchases for premiums, sales promotion,
inservices, training programs, fund-raisers or reselling at
1-800-497-4909 or e-mail
Info@QuillDriverBooks.com.

Did this book help you?
We'd love to hear how you
put this book to work .
E-mail us at Donna@WantItDoneRight.com.